D1169886

the**be** **with**factor

STUDENT GUIDE

Also by Bo Boshers:

*Student Ministry for the 21st Century*
(with Kim Anderson)

*Doing Life with God, Volumes 1 and 2*
(with Kim Anderson)

*Becoming a Contagious Christian Youth Edition*
(with Mark Mittelberg, Lee Strobel, and Bill Hybels)

*Vision Moments*
(with Keith Cote)

*G-Force: Taking Your Relationship with God
to a New Level*

Also by Judson Poling:

Walking with God series
(with Don Cousins)

Tough Questions series
(with Garry Poole)

Pursuing Spiritual Transformation series
(with John Ortberg and Laurie Pederson)

*Interpretation: Discovering the Bible for Yourself*
(from the Bible 101 series)

*Taking the Old Testament Challenge:
A Daily Reading Guide*
(with John Ortberg)

*The Journey: A Bible for the Spiritually Curious*
(general editor)

the**be** **with**factor
STUDENT GUIDE

six questions students
need to ask about
life with GOD

## bo boshers & judson poling

ZONDERVAN™

GRAND RAPIDS, MICHIGAN 49530 USA

WILLOW
Willow Creek Resources

ZONDERVAN.COM/
AUTHOR**TRACKER**

*The Be-With Factor Student Guide*
Copyright © 2006 by Willow Creek Association

Requests for information should be addressed to:
Zondervan, *Grand Rapids, Michigan 49530*

ISBN-10: 0-310-27161-4
ISBN-13: 978-0-310-27161-1

All Scripture quotations, unless otherwise indicated, are taken from the *Holy Bible: New International Version®*. NIV®. Copyright © 1973, 1978, 1984 by International Bible Society. Used by permission of Zondervan. All rights reserved.

Scripture quotations marked TNIV are taken from the *Holy Bible: Today's New International Version®*. TNIV®. Copyright © 2002, 2004 by International Bible Society. Used by permission of Zondervan. All rights reserved.

Scripture quotations marked NLT are taken from the *Holy Bible: New Living Translation*, copyright © 1996. Used by permission of Tyndale House Publishers, Inc., Wheaton, Illinois. All rights reserved.

All rights reserved. No part of this publication may be reproduced, stored in a retrieval system, or transmitted in any form or by any means—electronic, mechanical, photocopy, recording, or any other—except for brief quotations in printed reviews, without the prior permission of the publisher.

*Interior design by Mark Sheeres*

*Printed in the United States of America*

06 07 08 09 10 • 10 9 8 7 6 5 4 3 2 1

# contents

# introduction

**W**elcome to The Be-With Factor. The Be-With lifestyle is about "being-with" each other. It's about asking tough questions, listening to each other, and discovering *with others* what the Bible says about your life with God. It's also about hearing what those others have to say—everybody's point of view matters.

The best way to use this book is as a discussion guide for meetings with a mentor. That's one of the most important Be-With relationships you can have. A mentor can help you learn what being a Christ-follower is all about. But this book is also a great study guide for getting together with other students to study the Bible—if you have a small group leader, we recommend they purchase *The Be-With Factor* book which has a leader's guide to go along with these questions. Or if you just want to personally "be-with" God in a closer way, these questions and exercises can help strengthen your relationship with him.

Here are six "Big Questions" you might be asking—lots of students are. They're important questions, and how you answer them will determine how your relationship with God unfolds. So, no easy answers allowed. It's time to dig deep.

1. How Does God Show Me He's Real?
2. What Does God Want from Me?
3. What Purpose Does God Have for My Life?

4. Why Does It Matter What I Believe about God?
5. How Does God Help Me Stay Strong When Life Is Hard?
6. What Kind of People Does God Want in My Life?

Each question is the theme for the discussion, and there are several other questions and Bible verses to read to help you answer each Big Question. Take one lesson each week. If the conversation really gets going, you might not have time to discuss everything in the lesson, but that's a good thing. Don't worry about finishing every question in the study—the focus should be on your life with God, not on completing lessons. What's important is to be real about your relationship with God and the questions you have about your faith. You can always go back and finish the questions when you take time to be alone with God during the week.

# How Does God Show Me He's Real?

## big idea

God wants a personal relationship with us and has taken steps to make himself known.

## discussion questions

**1** What are some of your earliest memories of what you thought God was like?

**2** How has your view of God changed since then?

## read these passages from the Bible:

³When I look at the night sky and see the work of your fingers — the moon and the stars you have set in place — ⁴what are mortals that you should think of us, mere humans that you should care for us?

PSALM 8:3–4 NLT

¹The heavens declare the glory of God; the skies proclaim the work of his hands. ²Day after day they pour forth speech; night after night they display knowledge. ³There is no speech or language where their voice is not heard. ⁴Their voice goes out into all the earth, their words to the ends of the world.

PSALM 19:1–4

For since the creation of the world God's invisible qualities — his eternal power and divine nature — have been clearly seen, being understood from what has been made.

ROMANS 1:20

**3** How would you sum up what these verses are saying about God's message to humanity through his creation?

**4** How does God use his creation to speak to you personally?

God also speaks to us through the Bible, his written Word, and Jesus, his Word (message) made flesh.

## John 1:1 – 5 says:

¹In the beginning was the Word [Jesus], and the Word was with God, and the Word was God. ²He was with God in the beginning. ³Through him all things were made; without him nothing was made that has been made. ⁴In him was life, and that life was the light of all people. ⁵The light shines in the darkness, and the darkness has not overcome it.    TNIV

## Hebrews 1:1 – 3 says:

¹In the past God spoke to our ancestors through the prophets at many times and in various ways, ²but in these last days he has spoken to us by his Son, whom he appointed heir of all things, and through whom also he made the universe. ³The Son is the radiance of God's glory and the exact representation of his being, sustaining all things by his powerful word.    TNIV

**5** What do these passages teach us about Jesus' role in helping us understand God?

## now read John 1:10 – 14.

¹⁰He was in the world, and though the world was made through him, the world did not recognize him. ¹¹He came to that which was his own, but his own did not receive him. ¹²Yet to all who did receive him, to those who believed in his name, he gave the right to become children of God — ¹³children born not of natural descent, nor of human decision or a husband's will, but born of God. ¹⁴The Word became flesh and made his dwelling among us. We have seen his glory, the glory of the one and only [Son], who came from the Father, full of grace and truth.    TNIV

Many people saw and heard Jesus without being changed. In our day, too, lots of people know some facts about Jesus but are not among his followers.

**6** According to verses 12–13, how does someone go from being a creature *made* by God to a child *born* of God?

**7** Tell the story of when and how that happened for you.

In John 10:10, Jesus said, "I have come that they may have life, and have it to the full."

**8** What do you think keeps some people who follow Christ from having "life to the full" as he promised?

**9** What do you think is your role in making sure you experience the kind of abundant life Christ wants for you on a day-to-day basis?

## Here's one way Jesus put it:

"⁵I am the vine; you are the branches. If you remain in me and I in you, you will bear much fruit; apart from me you can do nothing. ⁶If you do not remain in me, you are like a branch that is thrown away and withers; such branches are picked up, thrown into the fire and burned. ⁷If you remain in me and my words remain in you, ask whatever you wish, and it will be done for you. ⁸This is to my Father's glory, that you bear much fruit, showing yourselves to be my disciples. ⁹As the Father has loved me, so have I loved you. Now remain in my love"

JOHN 15:5–9 TNIV

**10** Summarize in your own words the analogy Jesus used to explain this concept.

## scripture memory

God wants his Word to be deep in our hearts. A great way to make his Word part of our lives is to memorize parts of the Bible. We include a short verse each week so you can have some ready tools for God's Spirit to use to help you grow. Here's this week's verse:

"I have come that they may have life, and have it to the full."

JOHN 10:10

### how I see this verse applying to my life:

Share with others, or simply write a paragraph explaining how you see this verse affecting your daily life.

## personal challenge

When you meet, your mentor may occasionally give you a challenge or some "stretch"—an activity or behavior that gets you out of your comfort zone a bit as a way to grow. If that happens, jot it down here (and if you're not doing this study with a mentor, come up with your own challenge each week to help you apply what you have learned).

## my life

One way to understand and know God better is to read his Word. We need to read the Bible to feed our spiritual life just like we need to eat a little bit every day to feed our natural body (Matthew 4:4). It's also a good idea to keep a journal—a record of your thoughts, questions, prayers, and whatever else is going on in your life. At the end of every discussion, we'll give you some ideas you can think about and journal on between now and the next time you get together. There are some blank pages between each lesson you can use, or if you need more paper, start your own journal. Or, if you're a blogger, put it all out in cyberspace.

This week, notice the ordinary ways God reveals himself to you through nature, people, your conscience, and quiet promptings in your mind. At the end of each day, jot down how he showed you he was real that day. Be prepared to share your thoughts at the next meeting when you discuss "Big Question #2: What Does God Want from Me?"

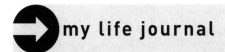

# my life journal

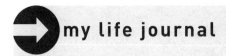**my life journal**

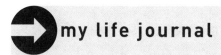

**my life journal**

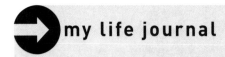my life journal

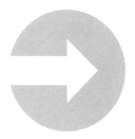

# What Does God Want from Me?

## big idea

Christianity is about a relationship with God based on grace and love; we obey him out of gratitude, not because we legalistically keep his rules out of fear.

## checking in

Did any interesting things come up in your journaling this week? Read or share a few thoughts from your journal.

Also, if you worked on a personal challenge this week, how did that go?

## discussion questions

**1** Describe a relationship where you weren't sure if you were "in" or "out" with the person.

**2** Why is it so hard to be close to someone who doesn't let you know where you stand with them?

Some people think a relationship with God is like that: he never lets you know where you stand, and at any moment he could turn on you if you step out of line. At times, you may also feel like you're not much of a friend to God.

**3** Why does this kind of uncertainty keep us from a close relationship with him?

### read Jesus' words:

[11]"I am the good shepherd. The good shepherd lays down his life for the sheep. [12]The hired hand is not the shepherd and does not own the sheep. So when he sees the wolf coming, he abandons the sheep and runs away. Then the wolf attacks the flock and scatters it. [13]The man runs away because he is a hired hand and cares nothing for the sheep. [14]I am the good shepherd; I know my sheep and my sheep know me — [15]just as the Father knows me and I know the Father — and I lay down my life for the sheep."

JOHN 10:11–15 TNIV

**4** What do you think Jesus wants his sheep to feel toward their shepherd?

## read these words of Jesus:

<sup>27</sup>"My sheep listen to my voice; I know them, and they follow me. <sup>28</sup>I give them eternal life, and they shall never perish; no one can snatch them out of my hand. <sup>29</sup>My Father, who has given them to me, is greater than all; no one can snatch them out of my Father's hand. <sup>30</sup>I and the Father are one."

JOHN 10:27–30

**5** According to Jesus, whose hands are on every one of his sheep?

**6** Why do you suppose Jesus stressed how secure his sheep are?

Reflect on this brief story: Once there was a tough coach who made a lot of demands on his players. He didn't seem to care about the team, and no one liked him. He would leave notes for his players, telling them what they'd done wrong and giving them lists of things he wanted them to do differently. The players would try to follow the coach's directions, but it always seemed like a lot of work, and they were constantly criticized for falling short.

Halfway through the season, that coach left and a new coach was hired in his place. The new guy was a strong coach but didn't demean the players. He was able to call the best out of the team, and he also generously encouraged them and really cared for each player. Everybody loved the new coach and they were glad to be rid of the old one.

One day, just before the last game of the season, a player found one of the old coach's "to do" notes in the back of his locker. He felt his face get hot with anger as he remembered what it was like to play under that tyrant, trying to please him to no avail. Yet as he read the note and its requirements, he realized that all the things the previous coach had written that he should do, *he was actually now doing*. He was playing harder than he'd ever played under the old coach, but he actually *wanted* to do those things on the list because of his trust, respect, and love for the new coach, and out of appreciation for how he was treated.

 What parallels can you make to this story and to how we relate to God?

## Jesus once told this story:

[10]"Two men went up to the temple to pray, one a Pharisee and the other a tax collector. [11]The Pharisee stood by himself and prayed: 'God, I thank you that I am not like other people — robbers, evildoers, adulterers — or even like this tax collector. [12]I fast twice a week and give a tenth of all I get.' [13]But the tax collector stood at a distance. He would not even look up to heaven, but beat his breast and said, 'God, have mercy on me, a sinner.' [14]I tell you that this man, rather than the other, went home justified before God. For all those who exalt themselves will be humbled, and those who humble themselves will be exalted."

Luke 18:10–14 TNIV

**8** What light does this shed on how people act when they think their relationship with God is based on performance rather than forgiveness and grace?

**9** Have you ever pretended to be righteous or been fake? Why did you think you had to do that?

Some people once asked Jesus, "What must we do to do the works God requires?" Jesus answered, "The work of God is this: to believe [that is, to trust] in the one he has sent" (John 6:28–29). The Greek word for "believe" in this passage includes the idea of "trust in, rely on, and cling to" (the New Testament was first written in Greek).

**10** In light of the meaning of this verse, what is the "first order of business" between God and us, according to Jesus?

**11** Why do we miss the mark if we try to follow the Ten Commandments or do other good things without first putting our trust in God's acceptance of us in Christ?

## scripture memory

Jesus answered, "The work of God is this: to believe in the one he has sent."

JOHN 6:29

### how I see this verse applying to my life:

Share with others, or simply write a paragraph explaining how you see the truth of this verse affecting your daily life.

## personal challenge

(From your mentor or on your own)

## my life

(To journal about this week) Reflect on these questions: "What is an area in which I have trouble trusting God? Why is trust hard for me in that area?" Be prepared to share your thoughts at the next meeting when you discuss "Big Question #3: What Purpose Does God Have for My Life?"

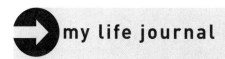

**my life journal**

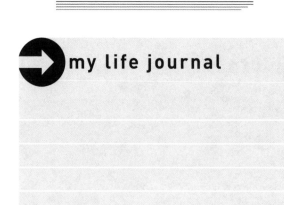
**my life journal**

**my life journal**

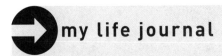
**my life journal**

**big question #3**

# What Purpose Does God Have for My Life?

## big idea

God has plans and desires for your life, and you're free to "dream big" because a big God wants to work through you.

## checking in

Did any interesting things come up in your journaling this week? Read or share a few thoughts from your journal.

Also, if you worked on a personal challenge this week, how did that go?

## discussion questions

**1** Describe a time when you saw or tried to use a tool that you couldn't figure out how to use correctly.

**2** What was it like when someone who knew what they were doing used the tool?

The prophet Isaiah said, "O LORD, you are our Father. We are the clay, you are the potter; we are all the work of your hand" (Isaiah 64:8).

**3** Knowing God made you as he did, what are some of the unique aspects of you, his special "pottery," that might indicate the plans he has for you and what he wants to do through your life?

The apostle Paul wrote, "For we are God's workmanship, created in Christ Jesus to do good works, which God prepared in advance for us to do" (Ephesians 2:10). The word for "workmanship" is the same root word that's behind the English word "poem."

**4** What's your reaction to the idea that you are God's poem?

**5** In the last part of Ephesians 2:10, it mentions that God has given much thought beforehand to the good works you will do. What does that advance preparation for your life mean to you personally?

Hundreds of years before Christ came to earth, the prophet Jeremiah recorded these words from God to his people: " 'For I know the plans I have for you,' declares the LORD, 'plans to prosper you and not to harm you, plans to give you hope and a future' " (Jeremiah 29:11). In that context, Israel was in exile far from home, but God was letting them know their hard times were not going to last.

**6** Because God's heart is the same toward you, how would you put into your own words, using your own name, the promise that is being given to you through the prophet Jeremiah?

"Come, follow me," Jesus once said to some men who'd been trying to catch some fish, "and I will send you out to fish for people" (Mark 1:17 TNIV). Jesus had a big change in mind for them. Notice that Jesus' role is to help us become certain kinds of people. Where we are, or what job we're doing is not as important as who we are and what kind of character we're developing. Notice Paul's words: "It is God's will that you should be sanctified: that you should avoid sexual immorality" (1 Thessalonians 4:3); he also wrote a little later, "Be joyful always; pray continually; give thanks in all circumstances, for this is God's will for you in Christ Jesus" (5:16 – 18). Now read all those verses aloud, but after the word "you," insert your name.

**7** If someone asked you, "What is God's will for me?" what do these verses say is part of the answer?

Centuries before Jesus, a writer in Psalms promised, "Delight yourself in the LORD and he will give you the desires of your heart" (Psalm 37:4).

**8** If the "desires of your heart" are what God wants to give you, then what does that say about an important part of how to find God's will for your life?

The famous fifth-century Christian leader Augustine once wrote, "Love God, and do as you please."

**9** How does that teaching line up with this verse? Can that be taken too far? Explain.

Jesus taught, "Whoever can be trusted with very little can also be trusted with much, and whoever is dishonest with very little will also be dishonest with much" (Luke 16:10).

**10** Based on the above teaching, if you wanted greater responsibilities or "advancement" in God's kingdom, what should you do first? Why do you think God set it up that way?

**11** How do you think this applies to God's leading you into the next step of his plan for your life?

## scripture memory

"For I know the plans I have for you," declares the LORD, "plans to prosper you and not to harm you, plans to give you hope and a future."

JEREMIAH 29:11

### how I see this verse applying to my life:

Share with others, or simply write a paragraph explaining how you see the truth of this verse affecting your daily life.

## personal challenge
(From your mentor or on your own)

## my life
(To journal about this week) Write a prayer asking God to show you some of the dreams he has for your life. Also, let God know some of the dreams you have in your own heart that you want to do for him. Be prepared to share your thoughts at the next meeting when you discuss "Big Question #4: Why Does It Matter What I Believe about God?"

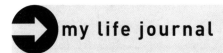

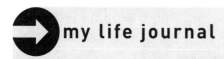**my life journal**

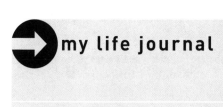

**my life journal**

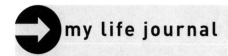

**my life journal**

# Why Does It Matter What I Believe about God?

## big idea

Spiritual beliefs have a direct correlation to how we live our lives, so it's important to examine our core beliefs to line them up with truth.

## checking in

Did any interesting things come up in your journaling this week? Read or share a few thoughts from your journal.

Also, if you worked on a personal challenge this week, how did that go?

## discussion questions

**1** Take exactly two minutes to write down as many words as you can to describe God. After you've done that, circle one or two of the words you think are most important.

**2** How would your life be different if God were not really this way?

### Jesus once told the following parable:

"²⁴Therefore everyone who hears these words of mine and puts them into practice is like a wise man who built his house on the rock. ²⁵The rain came down, the streams rose, and the winds blew and beat against that house; yet it did not fall, because it had its foundation on the rock. ²⁶But everyone who hears these words of mine and does not put them into practice is like a foolish man who built his house on sand. ²⁷The rain came down, the streams rose, and the winds blew and beat against that house, and it fell with a great crash."

MATTHEW 7:24–27

**3** Give an example of what Jesus is talking about.

**4** If Jesus and his words are so indispensable, how do you explain non-Christians whose lives seem to be going well?

Jesus warned, "Watch out that no one deceives you. For many will come in my name, claiming, 'I am the Messiah,' and will deceive many" (Matthew 24:4–5 TNIV). He added, "At that time if anyone says to you, 'Look, here is the Messiah!' or, 'There he is!' do not believe it. For false messiahs and false prophets will appear and perform great signs and wonders to deceive, if possible, even the elect. See, I have told you ahead of time. So if anyone tells you, 'There he is, out in the wilderness,' do not go out; or, 'Here he is, in the inner rooms,' do not believe it" (verses 23–26).

**5** Summarize in your own words what Jesus is warning us about in this passage. What are some examples of false Christs and false prophets in our day who make false spiritual claims or lead people astray in the name of religion?

Jesus had an interesting conversation with his disciples one day. He asked, "'Who do people say the Son of Man is?'["Son of Man" is one of the ways he identified himself.] They replied, 'Some say John the Baptist; others say Elijah; and still others, Jeremiah or one of the prophets.' 'But what about you?' he asked. 'Who do you say I am?' Simon Peter answered, 'You are the Messiah, the Son of the living God.'" Jesus liked that answer, and said, "'Blessed are you, Simon son of Jonah, for this was not revealed to you by flesh and blood, but by my Father in heaven'" (Matthew 16:13–17 TNIV).

He also argued with some religious leaders who opposed him and pronounced this judgment on their refusal to fully acknowledge that he was from God: "'You are from below; I am from above. You are of this world; I am not of this world. I told you that you would die in your sins; if you do not believe that I am the one I claim to be, you will indeed die in your sins' " (John 8:23–24).

**6** Based on what Jesus said, how important is it to rightly understand his identity?

One writer said there are basically four options for who Jesus was, historically speaking: he was either a liar (he made false claims for himself and knew it), a lunatic (made false claims for himself and really believed them), a legend (he never existed at all), or the Lord (God among us, just as he claimed).

**7** Based on Jesus' words, what might he say to someone who claimed, "I believe Jesus was a good man or maybe a prophet, but nothing more"?

When the religious leaders had a wrong view of the afterlife, Jesus corrected them and said, "You are in error because you do not know the Scriptures or the power of God" (Matthew 22:29).

**8** What two things led them into spiritual error, according to Jesus?

**9** How do these two things contribute to spiritual error in our day?

Someone has said, "Your 'testimony' is not what you were like before you became a Christ-follower; that's your history. Your testimony is how God is for you *all the time*." Go back to your list of words you made about God in question two.

**10** What words would you choose to describe the ways you sense God is personally *for* you? How important is it for you to see God this way?

## scripture memory

"I told you that you would die in your sins; if you do not believe that I am he, you will indeed die in your sins."

JOHN 8:24 TNIV

### how I see this verse applying to my life:

Share with others, or simply write a paragraph explaining how you see the truth of this verse affecting your daily life.

## personal challenge
(From your mentor or on your own)

## my life
(To journal about this week) Jesus clearly wants us to be immersed in the Scriptures and keenly aware of God's power (Matthew 22:29) so we can live well and be close to him. What are some ways you can increase your exposure to and appreciation for God's Word? Also, several times throughout the week, note a different aspect of God's power that you observe or value. Write down what you see and what it means to you. Be prepared to share your thoughts at the next meeting when you discuss "Big Question #5: How Does God Help Me Stay Strong When Life Is Hard?"

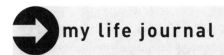 **my life journal**

**my life journal**

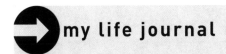

# my life journal

**my life journal**

# How Does God Help Me Stay Strong When Life Is Hard?

## big idea

We all have areas of temptation or weakness, and if we do not watch out for them, they will sideline us; we must know what those areas are and be vigilant to guard ourselves.

## checking in

Did any interesting things come up in your journaling this week? Read or share a few thoughts from your journal.

Also, if you worked on a personal challenge this week, how did that go?

## discussion questions

Experience shows we tend to sin in four big areas:

- Relational breakdowns (including lying, cheating, gossip, anger, excluding someone)
- Sexual misconduct (with a boyfriend/girlfriend, pornography, crass language and jokes)
- Financial wrongdoing (stealing, cheating, selfishness, materialism, greed)
- Addictions (drugs, alcohol, partying, eating disorders, perfectionism)

While there are several variations under each of these categories, we human beings tend to have our "fatal flaws" in these broad areas. We may not sin in any dramatic way, but lots of little compromises can add up to much pain and shame. If a person eventually does trash their life, it will usually follow one of these paths.

Relational breakdowns come in many flavors: explosive anger, betrayal of trust, disloyalty, abandonment, selfishness, using others for your own advantage, and jealousy, to name a few.

**1** Pick one of these breakdowns that you've experienced in some relationship in your life, either done to you or that you did to someone else, and tell what happened.

**2** What was the eventual outcome of that breakdown?

Here's a vivid description of sexual misconduct and its aftermath, right from the pages of Scripture:

> [21]With persuasive words she led him astray; she seduced him with her smooth talk. [22]All at once he followed her like an ox going to the slaughter, like a deer stepping into a noose [23]till an arrow pierces his liver, like a bird darting into a snare, little knowing it will cost him his life. [24]Now then, my sons, listen to me; pay attention to what I say. [25]Do not let your heart turn to her ways or stray into her paths. [26]Many are the victims she has brought down; her slain are a mighty throng. [27]Her house is a highway to the grave, leading down to the chambers of death.
>
> PROVERBS 7:21–27

Verse 21 describes one aspect of how seduction works, and verse 25, another. If you want to stay pure, it's much easier to avoid what comes *before* the act of sex than trying to stop sexual activity after passions are inflamed.

**3** What are those two "pre-sexual" activities to steer clear of?

**4** Have you ever used or had these used on you? Explain.

**5** Now, let's move on to financial wrongdoing. While outright theft may not be common among those you know, what are some ways greed, credit card misuse, copyright violations, or materialism can cause problems?

Let's propose a hypothetical future in which you reject God and choose to cast off all moral restraints.

**6** Go through each of the four areas mentioned at the beginning of this lesson and share what might be your most self-destructive tendency:

- Relational breakdowns


- Sexual misconduct


- Financial wrongdoing


- Addictions


If combating character weaknesses were easy, we'd all be successful at it. But the Bible is clear that these matters are a struggle—at times, it's like a war.

**7** Read the following verses. At the end of each set of verses put into your own words how God helps us as we fight this fight against sin.

> "I am the vine; you are the branches. If you remain in me and I in you, you will bear much fruit; apart from me you can do nothing."
>
> JOHN 15:5 TNIV

¹Therefore, I urge you, brothers and sisters, in view of God's mercy, to offer your bodies as a living sacrifice, holy and pleasing to God — this is true worship. ²Do not conform to the pattern of this world, but be transformed by the renewing of your mind. Then you will be able to test and approve what God's will is — his good, pleasing and perfect will.

ROMANS 12:1–2 TNIV

¹²The night is nearly over; the day is almost here. So let us put aside the deeds of darkness and put on the armor of light. ¹³Let us behave decently, as in the daytime, not in carousing and drunkenness, not in sexual immorality and debauchery, not in dissension and jealousy. ¹⁴Rather, clothe yourselves with the Lord Jesus Christ, and do not think about how to gratify the desires of the sinful nature.

ROMANS 13:12–14 TNIV

¹⁸Flee from sexual immorality. All other sins people commit are outside their bodies, but those who sin sexually sin against their own bodies. ¹⁹Do you not know that your bodies are temples of the Holy Spirit, who is in you, whom you have received from God? You are not your own; ²⁰you were bought at a price. Therefore honor God with your bodies.

1 CORINTHIANS 6:18–20 TNIV

No temptation has overtaken you except what is common to us all. And God is faithful; he will not let you be tempted beyond what you can bear. But when you are tempted, he will also provide a way out so that you can endure it.

1 CORINTHIANS 10:13 TNIV

13You, my brothers and sisters, were called to be free. But do not use your freedom to indulge the sinful nature; rather, serve one another humbly in love. 14For the entire law is fulfilled in keeping this one command: "Love your neighbor as yourself." 15If you keep on biting and devouring each other, watch out or you will be destroyed by each other. 16So I say, walk by the Spirit, and you will not gratify the desires of the sinful nature. 17For the sinful nature desires what is contrary to the Spirit, and the Spirit what is contrary to the sinful nature. They are in conflict with each other, so that you are not to do whatever you want. 18But if you are led by the Spirit, you are not under the law.

GALATIANS 5:13–18 TNIV

5Keep your lives free from the love of money and be content with what you have, because God has said, "Never will I leave you; never will I forsake you." 6So we say with confidence, "The Lord is my helper; I will not be afraid. What can human beings do to me?" 7Remember your leaders, who spoke the word of God to you. Consider the outcome of their way of life and imitate their faith.

HEBREWS 13:5–7 TNIV

7Submit yourselves, then, to God. Resist the devil, and he will flee from you. 8Come near to God and he will come near to you.

JAMES 4:7–8 TNIV

5In the same way, you who are younger, submit yourselves to your elders. All of you, clothe yourselves with humility toward one another, because, "God opposes the proud but shows favor to the humble and oppressed." 6Humble yourselves, therefore, under God's mighty hand, that he may lift you up in due time. 7Cast all your anxiety on him because he cares for you. 8Be alert and of sober mind. Your enemy the devil prowls around like a roaring lion looking for someone to devour. 9Resist him, standing firm in the faith, because you know that your fellow believers throughout the world are undergoing the same kind of sufferings.

1 PETER 5:5–9 TNIV

**8** Do you know any verses not on this list that help you resist temptation? What are they?

**9** The best of us will sometimes fall and commit the very sins we detest. What do the following verses teach we should do when that happens?

> For though a righteous man falls seven times, he rises again, but the wicked are brought down by calamity.
>
> PROVERBS 24:16

> Therefore confess your sins to each other and pray for each other so that you may be healed. The prayer of a righteous person is powerful and effective.
>
> JAMES 5:16 TNIV

[8]If we claim to be without sin, we deceive ourselves and the truth is not in us. [9]If we confess our sins, he is faithful and just and will forgive us our sins and purify us from all unrighteousness. [10]If we claim we have not sinned, we make him out to be a liar and his word is not in us. [1]My dear children, I write this to you so that you will not sin. But if anybody does sin, we have an advocate with the Father — Jesus Christ, the Righteous One. [2]He is the atoning sacrifice for our sins, and not only for ours but also for the sins of the whole world.

1 JOHN 1:8–2:2 TNIV

## scripture memory

If we confess our sins, he is faithful and just and will forgive us our sins and purify us from all unrighteousness.

1 JOHN 1:9

### how I see this verse applying to my life:

Share with others, or simply write a paragraph explaining how you see the truth of this verse affecting your daily life.

## personal challenge

(From your mentor or on your own)

## my life

(To journal about this week) Reflect on what would happen if you gave in to the "fatal flaw" you struggle with. What might your life look like in five years if you don't hold this flaw at bay? Write out a vivid description of your life trapped and dominated by that sin. Contrast that description with another portrait of your life completely and utterly free of that flaw—what might it look and feel like if you could stop it now? Remember, as a Christ-follower, you have been promised God's help to live life more freely and more fully. Be prepared to share your thoughts at the next meeting when you discuss "Big Question #6: What Kind of People Does God Want in My Life?"

# my life journal

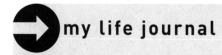

**my life journal**

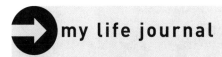 **my life journal**

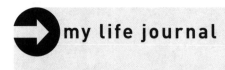

**my life journal**

# What Kind of People Does God Want in My Life?

## big idea

We must select circles of people around us who help us grow and give us ministry opportunities, while making sure we don't let friends lead us into sin.

## checking in

Did any interesting things come up in your journaling this week? Read or share a few thoughts from your journal.

Also, if you worked on a personal challenge this week, how did that go?

## discussion questions

**1**  "As iron sharpens iron, so one man sharpens another" (Proverbs 27:17). How would you put into your own words what this means?

**2**  What's an example from your life of how this works?

Paul wrote, "Therefore encourage one another and build each other up, just as in fact you are doing" (1 Thessalonians 5:11) and Hebrews 10:24–25 urges, "And let us consider how we may spur one another on toward love and good deeds, not giving up meeting together, as some are in the habit of doing, but encouraging one another—and all the more as you see the Day approaching" (TNIV).

**3**  Why do you think God wants us to play this kind of role in each other's lives as Christians—why isn't the Bible alone sufficient motivation or encouragement?

Just as people can build us up, they can also tear us down. "Do not be misled: 'Bad company corrupts good character'" (1 Corinthians 15:33).

**4**  Give an example of when you saw this happen in either your own life or that of someone you know.

Note the characteristics of the kinds of people who can wound us: "A perverse man stirs up dissension, and a gossip separates close friends; Do not make friends with a hot-tempered man, do not associate with one easily angered, or you may learn his ways and get yourself ensnared" (Proverbs 16:28; 22:24–25).

**5** How do you think we can show love to people like this, while at the same time not letting them do us harm?

In extreme cases, we might need to separate ourselves from certain people until they are willing to change. Here are the apostle Paul's words: "I wrote to you in my letter not to associate with sexually immoral people — not at all meaning the people of this world who are immoral, or the greedy and swindlers, or idolaters. In that case you would have to leave this world. But now I am writing to you that you must not associate with any who claim to be fellow believers but are sexually immoral or greedy, idolaters or slanderers, drunkards or swindlers. With such persons do not even eat" (1 Corinthians 5:9–11 TNIV). He also wrote, "Take special note of those who do not obey our instruction in this letter. Do not associate with them, in order that they may feel ashamed. Yet do not regard them as enemies, but warn them as fellow believers" (2 Thessalonians 3:14–15 TNIV).

**6** What does Paul say about the kind of person who presents the biggest threat to our spiritual well-being?

Jesus was called a "friend of sinners" (Matthew 11:19) and was scolded by religious leaders for hanging out with them at parties. "Then Levi held a great banquet for Jesus at his house, and a large crowd of tax collectors and others were eating with them. But the Pharisees and the teachers of the law who belonged to their sect complained to his disciples, 'Why do you eat and drink with tax collectors and "sinners"?' Jesus answered them, 'It is not the healthy who need a doctor, but the sick. I have not come to call the righteous, but sinners to repentance' " (Luke 5:29–32).

**7** What was Jesus' purpose in spending time with the "wrong" kind of people?

**8** How can we do like Jesus, yet not be drawn into the wrong actions that others may engage in?

## scripture memory

Do not be misled: "Bad company corrupts good character."
1 CORINTHIANS 15:33

### how I see this verse applying to my life:

Share with others, or simply write a paragraph explaining how you see the truth of this verse affecting your daily life.

## personal challenge
(From your mentor or on your own)

## my life
(To journal about this week) What two people would you like to thank for being a good influence on your life? (Think of at least one who is not a parent.) What are the qualities of the people that you value, and why do you consider those qualities so important? Who might include *your* name on such a list? How does that make you feel? Why? After you've written *about* those people who shaped you, why not write a note or an email *to* them?

## a final word
Congratulations on completing The Be-With Factor Student Guide: Six Questions Students Need to Ask About Life with God. Not everybody takes the time to delve into these kinds of tough questions; we hope you agree it was worth it. If you have been using this guide as part of a mentoring relationship, by now you see the value of having this person in your life. Be sure to let that person know what their "Be-With" investment in you has meant. If you've used this study as a group or personal enrichment tool, don't stop now. Keep discussing and studying the tough questions of life with an open mind—and an open Bible—so you can experience all God has for you as you follow him throughout your life's journey.

**my life journal**

# my life journal

**my life journal**

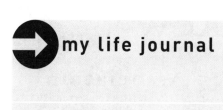

# Willow Creek Association

*Vision, Training, Resources for Prevailing Churches*

This resource was created to serve you and to help you build a local church that prevails. It is just one of many ministry tools that are part of the Willow Creek Resources® line, published by the Willow Creek Association together with Zondervan.

The Willow Creek Association (WCA) was created in 1992 to serve a rapidly growing number of churches from across the denominational spectrum that are committed to helping unchurched people become fully devoted followers of Christ. Membership in the WCA now numbers over 10,500 Member Churches worldwide from more than ninety denominations.

The Willow Creek Association links like-minded Christian leaders with each other and with strategic vision, training, and resources in order to help them build prevailing churches designed to reach their redemptive potential. Here are some of the ways the WCA does that.

- **A2: Building Prevailing Acts 2 Churches — Today** — an annual two-and-a-half day event, held at Willow Creek Community Church in South Barrington, Illinois, to explore strategies for building churches that reach out to seekers and build believers, and to discover new innovations and breakthroughs from Acts 2 churches around the country.

- **The Leadership Summit** — a once a year, two-and-a-half-day conference to envision and equip Christians with leadership gifts and responsibilities. Presented live at Willow Creek as well as via satellite broadcast to over one hundred locations across North

America, this event is designed to increase the leadership effectiveness of pastors, ministry staff, volunteer church leaders, and Christians in the marketplace.

• **Ministry-Specific Conferences**—throughout each year the WCA hosts a variety of conferences and training events—both at Willow Creek's main campus and offsite, across the U.S., and around the world—targeting church leaders and volunteers in ministry-specific areas such as: evangelism, small groups, preaching and teaching, the arts, children, students, women, volunteers, stewardship, raising up resources, etc.

• **Willow Creek Resources**®—provides churches with trusted and field-tested ministry resources in such areas as leadership, evangelism, spiritual formation, spiritual gifts, small groups, stewardship, student ministry, children's ministry, the use of the arts-drama, media, contemporary music—and more.

• **WCA Member Benefits**—includes substantial discounts to WCA training events, a 20 percent discount on all Willow Creek Resources®, *Defining Moments* monthly audio journal for leaders, quarterly *Willow* magazine, access to a Members-Only section on WillowNet, monthly communications, and more. Member Churches also receive special discounts and premier services through WCA's growing number of ministry partners—Select Service Providers—and save an average of $500 annually depending on the level of engagement.

For specific information about WCA conferences, resources, membership, and other ministry services contact:

**Willow Creek Association**
P.O. Box 3188
Barrington, IL 60011-3188
Phone: 847-570-9812
Fax: 847-765-5046
www.willowcreek.com

# G-Force
## Taking Your Relationship with God to a New Level

### *Bo Boshers*

Ever feel tired of trying REALLY HARD to be a Christian?

Being a Christ-follower isn't about trying really hard; it's about training to be more like Jesus so he can transform you into the person he made you to be. *G-Force* shows you how.

The "Five Gs" of *G-Force* are markers or guides for your spiritual journey. They are designed to help take the guesswork out of what it really means to be a fully devoted follower of Christ—to live like Jesus would if he were in your place. In personal devotions and weekly small group gatherings, you'll learn about

**Grace:** Move beyond religious rules and regulations and learn how to live in God's grace—then learn how to share this grace with others.

**Growth:** Discover how spiritual practices can bring you closer to the heart of God.

**Groups:** Experience an authentic community where you will learn what it means to know and be known—to have real and intimate friendships throughout your life.

**Gifts:** Identify your spiritual gifts and dedicate them to serving God—then watch how God uses your gifts to impact the world in amazing ways.

**Good Stewardship:** Trust God with all your resources and discover what it means to live with freedom and generosity.

In each session you'll be challenged to think about what you really believe and learn how to have a deeper relationship with God and with others. Once you discover the power of G-Force, you learn that being a Christian is ultimately about Christ with you and within you, guiding and empowering you to become more like him.

Softcover: 0-310-24446-3

*Pick up a copy today at your favorite bookstore!*

**ZONDERVAN**™
GRAND RAPIDS, MICHIGAN 49530 USA
WWW.ZONDERVAN.COM

**WILLOW**
Willow Creek Resources

# Student Ministry for the 21st Century

## Transforming Your Youth Group into a Vital Student Ministry

*Bo Boshers with Kim Anderson*

Why settle for a "youth group" when you can build a dynamic student ministry that keeps more and more students coming—and keeps them growing!

From the director of Student Impact, one of the country's largest and most effective student ministries, here is a clear, step-by-step approach that takes you for a quantum leap beyond merely

| Maintaining a Youth Group ... | to Building a Student Ministry |
|---|---|
| Activity-driven | Purpose-driven |
| Unclear vision | Clear vision |
| Inward focus, content with the "clique" | Outward focus, compassion for lost people |
| Minimum growth | Consistent growth |
| Songs and games | Worship and prayer |
| Keeps the traditions | Evaluates for effectiveness |
| "Babysitting" | Impacting the world |

Softcover: 0-310-20122-5

*Pick up a copy today at your favorite bookstore!*

ZONDERVAN™

GRAND RAPIDS, MICHIGAN 49530 USA

WWW.ZONDERVAN.COM

WILLOW

Willow Creek Resources

We want to hear from you. Please send your comments about this book to us in care of zreview@zondervan.com. Thank you.

**ZONDERVAN**™

GRAND RAPIDS, MICHIGAN 49530 USA

ZONDERVAN.COM/
AUTHOR**TRACKER**